I CAN'T IMAGINE

By
Jo Chamberlain
&
Alexandra Carr

Table of Contents

A Tribute To God's Servant… Candy	7
-1- The Journey Begins	
Are You In A Valley?	10
God Loves You	11
Forever Is Just A Call Away	12
Call Jesus	13
Come Jesus	14
Jesus Is Forever	15
A Celebration Of Life	16
He Is Risen, Indeed	17
He Is Living	18
Are You Ready For Jesus?	19
Wishing And Waiting	20
Joy To The World, He Lives	21
Side By Side	22
Special Shepherds	23
Shepherds	24
Fathers	25
Harvest With Love	26
I Can't Imagine	27
Thank You Lord	28
Don't Forget To Thank The Lord	29
Because We Love You Lord	30
Be Always Thanking God	31
Adaptation Of Psalm 136	32
-2- Her Walk Continues	
Do You Know My Friend?	35
My Best Friend	36

Table of Contents (cont.)

Fire Up	37
Count It All Joy	38
Which Way Will You Go?	39
Tell Them	40

-3- The End of Jo's Journey

Lately	42
Tomorrow?	43
Red Light	44
What A Sunset!	45
My Choice Is Made	46
"A Merry Heart Doeth Good Like A Medicine"	47
Still Praising	48
Always Praise Him	49
Help Me Lord	50
Last Stop	51
Please Lord	52
"Remember Now Your Creator In The Days Of Your Youth"	53
Call	54
Come Now	55
What A Deal	56
Only Trust Jesus	57
Be Still	58
No Need For Panic	59
It's Your Choice	60
Happy Anniversary With Love	61
Little Denton: Jefferson	63

Table of Contents (cont.)

Remember God Hates Sin, He Loves You	64
Averse In A Fish	65
Oh Lord, You Seasoned The Earth	68
Have You Talked To My Friend?	69
America Is Still Free	70
Do We Need A New Wardrobe?	71
A Real Gift Of Love	72
Birth Of Our Messiah	73
He Is Love	74
The Manger And The Cross	75
Oh Happy Day	76
What Do You Say?	77
The Walk	78
The Rain Will Dry Up So Should We!	79
Written December 1994	80
My First Day in Heaven Back cover	82

The poems and essays in this book are written by an absolutely incredible woman! Her name was Jewell Edna Chamberlain, Jo to those who knew her, and she was my Grandmother. She meant the world to me, and to a lot of people who simply just met her. I know that no one could ever fill her shoes, or hold her pen in this case. Jo was a strong believer in Christ and she let everyone know it.

Jo's Christian life was dedicated first and foremost to God! Next on her list was her church, and her family. Not a second went by that Jo didn't think about Jesus, what He meant to her, and how she can spread His word. This is why she started writing poetry dedicated to her Lord Jesus Christ.

Jo had a large church family that absolutely adored her. These poems were mostly written for them and the monthly newsletter that they put out. She would often take poem requests from the pastors for each month's newsletter.

She spent every Tuesday cleaning the sanctuary and on every Friday she folded the bulletins for Sunday's service. Jo loved having lunch with the pastors and other staff members there. I believe that was her bonding time with all of them. It was her own therapy, her way to deal with day to day trials.

My incredibly wonderful Grandmother went to be with her Lord Jesus Christ on March 2, 2004. That was the day she was truly born and can now spend her days with her maker. I know that she is now happier than she has ever been.

Here is a poem that my mother, Candy Minus, wrote for my grandma. For several years my grandma cleaned the sanctuary on Tuesdays (and later Fridays). She would pick up bulletins and other garbage left behind, restock envelopes, straighten hymnals and sharpen pencils. One Tuesday she found a "scrap" piece of paper in the hymnal rack addressed to her. The paper contained the following "message" from my mom.

A Tribute To God's Servant

Dear Mom,

It's a wonderful blessing to find you here today. Not just because of what you're doing here but because of why you're here. You are a member here (at Grace Evangelical Church) and you take your membership serious. This is God's house and His family is here all around you. You love God and He gives you peace here. I love you and I'm so proud of you. Thank you for giving to the Lord.

Pick up all the candy wrappers,
Sharpen pencils too.
God has a sharp eye on you
And His arms are wrapped around you too.

Pick up bits on the carpet,
Line the Bibles straight in the pew.
God's love can be seen this Tuesday
Right in the heart of you!

Visit all your loved ones,
Wish Todd a blessing today.
Watch over Jeff as he practices,
But please don't help him play.
Give Jim a hug and a pretty smile,
Help our Jan file awhile.
If it's Pastor Dave you see,
Tell him we love him, and to pray for "We".

Candy Minus

-1-
The Journey Begins

This first group of poems was written in the beginning of Jo's walk with Christ. She took a lot of requests from her pastors and did a lot of research in her Bible before she put her words to paper. You will see that Jo continuously asks for you to come to Christ. She was just coming to know Him and wanted you to go along with her on this awesome journey. It is a wonderful trip bursting with Jo's love and devotion to Christ. Now, you can take this journey with her. Sit back and enjoy the ride.

Are You In A Valley

Have you ever been through your Valley of Baca?
A valley is a place where you are down oh so very low.
Were your tears falling in torrents,
    And did your heart feel all broken?
Did you not call out to Our Lord,
    With prayers that needed to be spoken?
His living Presence is our greatest joy,
He can help us to grow in strength, grace, and glory.
He is always waiting and longing for us to call upon Him,
The miracles He can perform are life's greatest story.
If you are wandering, broken hearted
    Right now through your Valley of Tears,
        Find Jesus,
            He can calm all your fears.
As you go on your journey seeking His aid,
Remember, He died on that old rugged Cross.
He arose, He lives,
    For all our sins He has already paid.
Jesus is not very far,
    If you call out to Him,
        He will come where you are.
Do it now, "CALL," tell Him your sorrow.
For all of us,
    Without Him as Our Savior,
        We may have no tomorrow.
So you see, we must have an _active_ faith,
    If you need Him,
        Seek and Call – He will answer.

God Loves You

When nothing seems to make sense,
And your troubles seem like more than you can bear,
Take your eyes off your trials and look to God in your despair.
God can and will help you,
It has already been done.
To save us from dying because of our sin,
On an old cross on a hill, He spared not His only Son.
So no matter what happens to us,
And no matter where we are,
We can never be lost to His love.
Trials should not drive us away from Him,
But they should bring us ever closer to Our Father above.
God delivered Jesus up for us all.
Why would He not, with Him, also freely give us all things we need?
Remember His time is not always our time.
No matter how much we plead.
Knowing this I agree with Habakkuk (3:17-18)
That we that have faith in God's Love,
Should wait and take joy in the God of our salvation,
In His time He will act from above.
Don't take any steps away from your Savior,
Hold His love so close in your heart,
He will help you – from your trust He will not depart.
Wait on God! He loves you!

Forever Is Just A Call Away

When I sing about the old rugged cross,
My eyes fill up with tears and my heart burns with love.
Just remembering that is where sweet Jesus died for me.
I also know He arose from His tomb,
And someday His loving face I'm gonna see!
Do you know Jesus? He died for you too!
He is waiting and longing. Yes, I said longing,
To hear, especially, from you!
Do you know He really died for us all?
I know it's hard to take in,
But He died to pay for <u>our</u> sin.
If you are still saying,
"I'm not a sinner!"
My brother or sister,
I say, "Think again!"
We are <u>all</u> conceived in sin,
But for everlasting live we need to be born again.
Jesus can fix that!
I tell you He is waiting for your call.

I BEG YOU – CALL JESUS!

Call Jesus

March 2, 1995

Jesus is pleading for you to call Him, you know?
Do you know He truly does miss you so?
Do you know Jesus is bending low to hear you call out His name?
Call Now!
Time is of the essence,
All excuses are lame.
Do you know with Him,
Broken hearts can be mended?
Do you know with Him,
Your sins can be rescinded?
He esteems those who are humble and contrite in spirit,
The ones who tremble at His Word when they hear it!
Do you know He is preparing a special "place" for you on High?
That is a promise. Believe it!
We will have a joyful party with Jesus, one day,
Up there in the sky.
I'm going to be at that party,
My plans are all laid.
You, call out to Jesus,
And get your reservation made!
He is waiting to hear from YOU!
Please call Jesus!

Come Jesus

Rejoice! The Lord is near!
If we have given our lives to the Lord,
We have nothing to fear.
It is not that we HAVE to pray,
We GET to pray.
With thanksgiving, we "get" to present our requests to Him,
At any time on any day.

Rejoice! The Lord is near!
You can do everything through Him who gives you
strength.
His power is able to carry you to any length.
We need to thank Him for things we often take for granted,
The sun, the rain, the moon and the stars,
And all the lovely things He has planted.
What an awesome Savior, that He does love us so,
He took all our sins with Him, and did, to Golgotha go.
Yes, He died to save us sinners,
On a rugged cross, alone.
He paid it all!
For our sins He did atone.
But that's not the end of this story!

Rejoice! The Lord is near!
He arose from His tomb,
Now He is awaiting us up in Glory.
He is coming back,
His promises are true.
If you are still standing up for Jesus,
He is coming back for you!

Come, Jesus!

Jesus Is Forever
(January 1996)

Jesus is so eagerly seeking your heart,
Don't turn Him away call Him today.
See He is just over there, He's coming this way-
No, please don't run away. Stay and meet Jesus.

I stayed and met Jesus, He is in charge of my life.
No, everything is not perfect, but He helps me with the strife.
Just knowing He is near quiets my heart in moments of unrest,
I will always trust My Jesus, He passes every test.
Why He decided to take me to the hospital this past Christmas Eve is unknown,
I was in a state of desperate illness, but His presence there was also known.
Total darkness I remember.
No sound, no light did show.
Then finally I remember coming back into the light,
Brought back by prayers from everyone I know.
You were all so wonderful, Jeff was so dedicated,
Our Grace is a beautiful place.
In the light of Pastor Dave's message Sunday,
I may understand why I'm back in this human race.
He asked, "Can Christmas Wait?"
Did I, or did Jesus make that decision
That I should stay here and do my best for Him?
Paul stayed. I can do it too!
Yes, I believe that Christians can wait, how about you?

I know that Jesus is so eagerly seeking your heart,
He's not very far – just over there.
If He calls out to you, please don't run away.
Stay, and meet Jesus.
You will never be sorry!
He loves you!

I Love You, Jesus.

A Celebration Of Life

Oh, God, instill in my heart a new song.
Implant in my mind, for that song,
New words to sing.
Soon is coming a Holy celebration,
To remind us that Jesus is living,
And He is Our King.
Yes, He died to pay for all our sin.
And, as He promised,
He arose from the tomb.
And He really did come back again.
      Hallelujah!
Perhaps we need to feel the pain that He felt on the cross
that day,
To realize just how much He gave to pay.
Isaiah said,
      "He is our Messiah,
      He is our Wonderful Counselor.
      He is Exceptional,
            Distinguished, and without peer.
      He is our Mighty God that we hold so dear.
      He is our Everlasting Father, and timeless.
      He is our Prince of Peace,
            And His love for us will never cease."
Our Savior HAS come and He IS coming again.
Not forgetting His promises for thee and me.
So my new song will be about a celebration of live
Yes! His Life!
I wonder, what will your song be?

He Is Risen, Indeed

Jesus! Our Holy Lamb –
My heart is filled with so much love,
Every time I remember Him.
And it is so dolorous to me that He was crucified,
Tho' He was guilty of not one sin.
Even as He was dying while nailed on that old cross,
He begged Our Father to forgive our sins,
So we would not be forever lost.
Nothing at that time would have stopped Him from dying,
Because He had come down to Earth <u>to save us.</u>
Many people try to be "stars" here on Earth,
However, God tells us how we can be eternal "stars."
Life in Glory with Him can truly be ours.
If we are wise we will shine like the brightness of Glory
As we lead sinners to righteousness telling them –
To accept God's "Life Saving Story."
All Praises to His Name, He is near!
Do you know Him?
Call out to Him – He will come!
I pray:
"Sweet Jesus, just stretch out Your arms and draw Your lost lambs all close.
Save them I pray, save them today!
Tomorrow may be too late!"
I love You Jesus!

This next poem was written and read for the Easter service in 1994. Jo also gave her testimony that Sunday.

He Is Living

Let us celebrate our Savior,
He died that we might live.
Jesus loved us so much,
He gave all that He could give.
He was nailed upon a cross,
Tho' guilty of no sin was He.
Who would not care about this Savior,
When He would die for you and me?
At His Last Supper, Jesus drew His disciples near,
Could they truly have understood everything?
They didn't seem to have sufficient fear.
One disciple understood and left the supper,
The whereabouts of Jesus to betray.
All the others vowed to keep the watch,
And with our Savior to stay.
They went to Gethsemane planning to rest and pray.
Jesus must have felt so lonely, they all kept falling asleep.
Even today, do we Christians fall asleep
In our devotion to Him to keep?
What about Peter, who swore by Him to stay?
But when the soldiers came for Jesus,
Even Peter ran away!
How lonely for Jesus! Let's never leave Him.
Let's call Him every day.
Loneliness! So alone was He when they Him on that cross.
Everytime I remember this,
My heart feels such a loss.
But loss is not why He did it. It was gain for us that He died.
Joy! His innocent blood washed away all our sin,
If we choose we can walk by His side.
Because Jesus <u>AROSE</u> from His lonely tomb,
Just as He promised to do.
Hallelujah! He is living! Hi is coming back! Are you ready?
I choose Jesus, how about you?
Please celebrate Jesus, He can do anything for you.
He can clean out the cobwebs of sin from your heart,
And make it like brand new.
He is listening, watching, and waiting for our call,
I will call Him, will you?
Dedicated to Jesus, who LIVES!

Are You Ready For Jesus?

How would it be for you and for me,
If Jesus should come today?
As for me, I've chosen Him as my Savior,
I love Him with all my heart and soul.
I know my name is written in the Book of Life
For Jesus to behold.
Are you ready? Or do you really believe this life is all there can be?
He has said He is already preparing wonderful things for thee,
To find that truth just read the Bible and see.
God, The Father, sent His only Son to Earth to be our Savior,
He grew up among men, and though innocent of sin,
Jesus died on a cross for us all one day.
He arose again, and said He would come back again.
Yes, He will return in all His Glory to gather His children home,
So don't delay, accept Him today,
Dear loved one, don't turn Him away.
For how would it be for you and for me,
If Jesus should come today?

Wishing And Waiting

I wish I had been there with Jesus in that garden,
I could have knelt at His feet and begged for His pardon.
I wish I could have stopped Judas,
But that was not meant to be.
Jesus was going to die for you and for me.
I wish I had been near Jesus that day at the Cross,
I could have told Him I love Him, and how my heart felt such a loss.
Oh, but I wish I had been there when they rolled back that stone,
And Jesus arose and His full Glory shone.
Praise our Savior, Hallelujah, He is now living on High,
He will come back for us in some sweet by and by.
Wishes are nice, oh what a great reverie,
Untold is the joy in our hearts there will be,
When He finally comes, and His loving face we WILL see!

Joy To The World, He Lives

The good news on this Easter celebration –
We do know our Savior still lives!
Not only is He still waiting on High for us,
Our Savior still forgives
Remember:
Sin is the onset of soul inflammation,
And sooner or later will cause devastation.
Failing to accept Christ as ones Savior at all,
Will definitely be the first step to our downfall.
Christ is the only savior that God ever gave,
Without Him Heaven can never be attained,
All He need say is, "I never knew you,"
And that sinner's fate will be forever sealed.
No one, not anyone's life can be repealed.
For now – it 's a lovely Easter, Jesus is still waiting,
He is longing for all of us to call,
If you don't know Him, please won't you hurry?
He never sleeps, call Him any time at all,
Now, this moment, just don't be too late!
Don't let the answer, "I never knew you,"
Be your final fate.
I know my Savior, and my heart gets excited,
Because I know He is listening when I call.
He is so loving and faithful,
No problem is too big for Jesus at all.
However, don't cry for His pardon unless
You are willing to repent and come to Him.
Jesus is the only One able to erase all your sin.
On that awesome morning so very long ago,
Jesus died on that Old Cross to pay for all our sin.
So why don't you put your trust in Jesus?
One day He will open Heaven's Gate and tell you,
"Enter In"!

Mother's Day Essay
*Jo wrote this special tribute to Moms for Mother's Day
1995*

<u>Side By Side</u> was used for the Mother's Day church newsletters in 1991 and May of 1995.

<u>Side By Side</u>

Mothers are so special, they really have two sides.
Sometimes she is a soft as a petal on a rose.
When you are sick, she is always there to hold you close and say a prayer.
When you are hurt, she will soothe the spot and wipe away your tears.
When you are frightened, she will chase away those fears.
Mom is always there!

Sometimes Mothers can be tough like a cactus in the desert,
      Lovely, but tough.
Many times in our lives "wrong" gets out of hand.
Mom doesn't love you any less when she has to reprimand.
Perhaps you think she is just being mean.
Not true!
In her love for you, it's for your well-being.
She's there for you.

So tell Mom today just how much you really love her!
One more thing, whisper to her something special just for her ears.
She will hold that treasure in her heart through all the coming years.

God's rose and cactus can work side by side.
Just look at your Mom!

Special Shepherds

God made mothers His Shepherds down here on Earth.
Mother tends His flock of little lambs even before their birth.
Mother carries them ever so close to her heart,
And then she teaches them to walk.
Everything goes really great, but then she teaches them to talk.
Now, that can be a barrel of fun
Until maybe some little "no-no" pops out.
Oh my, then it's "Sweetie, never say that word,
The pastor could be about."
But the pastor has already learned those words,
And he knows these Shepherds are following God's plan-
To guide His little lambs with love,
And lead them through this land.
Striving never to let even one lamb fall or stray.
Mothers can tell them about God every day.
And mothers can teach them how to always pray.
Alas, comes a certain time in life,
When mothers have to let their lambs go,
"Please bless mothers, God, when that happens.
And let their guidance show.
Amen

Shepherds

From the beginning –
Mothers were special creations sent from up above,
God so loves little children that He gives them to mothers to nurture and love.
God chose Mary of Nazareth as the Mother of Jesus,
Mary gave Him life on Earth as her precious son.
Thirty some years later she watched Him die as her savior
To pay for the sins of everyone.
He gave His mother and all of us a chance for eternal living,
Why would we not love this Jesus,
When for us His own life He was so generously giving?
What a blessing for mothers that He trusts them so much
To watch over His lambs so young and so dear!
Don't you know sometimes He has some disappointments,
That must cause Him to shed many a tear?
Yes, mothers are special creations,
Shepherds if you please.
They do love and tend Gods beloved children,
And for His guidance they pray fervently –
Oh yes, and much of that fervent praying is done down on their knees!
So thank God for your mother,
Your shepherd.
Always treat her with kindness and love.
Remember she is a special creation,
From Our Father in Heaven Above!

Fathers

God is our Holiest Father in Heaven and on Earth,
He knows us so well, even before our birth.
Can we any way imagine how we are so intricately designed?
He knows our soul, our heart, and even our mind.
He is so Holy, so almighty, so full of grace and caring.
With our father down here, our life, He is sharing.

Our fathers here on Earth are so important to our life,
They share in our birth, our good things, and our strife.
They love us so much they will often sacrifice,
Keeping much less for them, to make our lives easier and nice.
We need to pray they love God with all their heart and soul,
If they instill that love in us it will be like pure gold.

Our Holiest Father is watching, He never sleeps,
It is a vigil that He will eternally keep.
Remember He sees you and your dad.
Try never to do anything that will make either of them sad!
Love your dad and honor him all of his days.
Ask our Heavenly Father to bless fathers, always!

Harvest With Love

Summer is ending,
Harvest is near,
The crops we've been tending
Are ever so dear.
Some "vines" are young and tender,
Others more mature,
All dearly loved by our Lord
We are sure
The "cuttings" are cared for
Until proper times,
When they grow roots
And develop into vines.

We harvesters must be diligent,
And let not our vines decay.
Our fruits grow in clusters,
We want none to fall away.
We must tend souls for our Lord
In the very same way!

Summer has faded,
It's time to make haste,
Let us gather up our fruits,
There is no time to waste.

We give up the bounty to You,
Lord as we pray,
That You will have a beautiful,
Happy harvest day!

I Can't Imagine

What did Thanksgiving Day mean to me before I knew Jesus Christ? Probably just cooking a turkey dinner and being happy if it was edible. Seriously tho, I have always loved Thanksgiving Day and I'm certain I mouthed the words "Thank God" when the dinner turned out delicious and it usually did! Only "lip service" at that time, but He was always there. Oh, maybe He stepped out now and then and the potatoes got watery or the gravy got lumpy, the rolls burned or the pumpkin pie sank, but not too often. I wasn't a total disbeliever. If one of our guests was a "good soul" they were asked to say "Grace" and that was duly appreciated.

It makes me sad now when I think how I ignored Jesus then, and I love Him so much now that I can't imagine wanting to do anything without Him in it! Everything is not always Hallelujah great, but every day is Thanksgiving Day for all my "good and plenty"! Thank you Lord!

Thank You Lord

I just want to thank the Lord for leading me to Grace,
I see so much love here in every blessed face.
I just want to thank the Lord for our special music and our choir,
They always give me a Hallelujah feeling I require.
I just want to thank the Lord for Dave, our Pastor,
He's truly gifted in giving us the Word from our Master.
For everyone and everything at Grace,
I just want to say – Thank You Lord!

The above poem was written in 1990 and in 1994 Jo added this:
Thank you Lord, it just gets better all the time! It could be a little "taste of Heaven."

Don't Forget To Thank The Lord

Thanksgiving Day is drawing nigh,
Do enjoy the football, turkey, and pumpkin pie.
All that is great, we have no doubt.
But thanking our Lord is what we should be about.
Thank the Lord for His loving blessings to you,
Thank the Lord for His amazing grace too.
Thank the Lord for the Holy Spirit
Who counsels and comforts us in our tears and strife.
Thank Jesus, who died for our sins
That we might have life.
Thank Him, He is our Savior, and He is coming again,
For He is The Way.
Don't you just know that His next coming will be –
THE perfect Thanksgiving Day!?

I thank the Lord for all of you!

Because We Love You Lord

We thank You for your loving kindness,
To forgive us of our sin,
We thank You for Jesus, our Savior
We know He is coming back again.

We thank You for the Cross,
Lest we should ever forget how much it cost You.
Every time we think of it,
Our love it will always renew.

We thank You that You hold us close,
When a sorrow comes into our heart.
We thank You that if we steadfastly follow you –
From us You will never depart.

We thank You for our daily bread
That Your love so generously gives.
And, oh Lord, we thank You again for Jesus,
Because we know our Savior lives!

Be Always Thanking God

Our God is a Great God,
Come before Him with a thankful heart.
Thank Him that you can do all things,
Because of strength to you He will impart.
Thank Him that His Word is wonderful and true,
Stay very close to Him, oh so close,
No matter how bad the world seems to you!
Thank Him that if we obey His laws,
Real happiness we can achieve.
He truly is the only way,
And that we must believe.
Thank Him for Jesus, our Savior,
He came down to die for all our sin,
Jesus, Jesus, Jesus – His love knows no end!
Thank Him for the best news that you ever could receive,
Yes, and it came from an old graveyard –
"Jesus Has Risen"
That news you can believe!

So, Thank Him again for Jesus,
We know Jesus is coming down again.
It may be soon, it may be a long time,
We never know when the "coming" will be.
If we keep living our lives for Jesus,
His Loving Face we are going to see.
Thank Him for His promise
Of an eternal Home on High.
While we are awaiting His arrival
We must be bringing in may new lambs
For our Shepherd in the Sky.

Thank you God!

Adaptation of Psalm 136
(Written as a responsive reading for a multi-church Thanksgiving service)

Give thanks to the Lord, for His Name and His Word is exalted above everything.
> His love endures forever.

Give Thanks to the Lord for coming into our lives, and for His kindness' that are always offered.
> His love endures forever.

Give Thanks to the Lord for our delightful inheritance, and we will see His face.
> His love endures forever.

Give Thanks to the Lord that in His blood we have been freed.
> His love endures forever.

Give Thanks to the Lord, celebrate His salvation everyday.
> His love endures forever.

Give Thanks to the Lord for His unfailing love, only He could design, is ours.
> His love endures forever.

Give Thanks to the Lord for His grace that never fails from age to age.
> His love endures forever.

Give Thanks to the Lord for His goodness, and His mercy that never runs out.
> His love endures forever.

Give Thanks to the Lord for prayers that are answered, we can lean on Him.
> His love endures forever.

Give Thanks to the Lord for the Holy Spirit who counsels and comforts us.
> His love endures forever.

Give Thanks to the Lord for our suffering as we remember He suffered too.
> His love endures forever.

Give Thanks to the Lord that He never sleeps, He is always watching over us.

Adaptation of Psalm 136 *(Cont.)*

His love endures forever.
Give Thanks to the Lord for our wealth – great or small.
    His love endures forever.
Give Thanks to the Lord for the Heavens and the Earth, as we listen to their symphony.
    His love endures forever.
Give Thanks to the Lord for the Cross, lest we should ever forget how much He loves us.
    His love endures forever.
Give Thanks to the Lord, praise Him, He is our Holiest Father on Earth and Heaven.
    His love endures forever.

-2-
Her Walk Continues

As Jo's journey goes deep, her pleading goes even deeper. She wants you to feel the wonderful joy that she is feeling only by knowing Christ. Jo has now put every thought, action, and emotion into her devotion. Let's continue with Jo's walk through her life and her wonderful poetry.

Do You Know My Friend?

Jesus is the dearest friend I have,
I cannot bear it when I grieve him,
He is the very first love in my heart,
When I cried out to him, He came to my rescue.
He is truly my shield and my rampart,
I know that because I love him,
And I acknowledge his name,
He will command his angels to protect me,
From any terror, plagues, or shame.
If you don't know Jesus, my Savior, today
I beg you to change that, because He is he Only Way!
Call to Him, tell Him your sorrows, pain your sin-
Ask His forgiveness and wait upon Him!
His decisions are not always what we deserve, you and I,
But He died for our sins, we never have to die!
Eternal life, and loving Jesus is what this is all about,
Each time I remember, I just want to shout- Hallelujah!
Please seek Jesus- He fill find you.

My Best Friend

Here on earth it this year of Our Lord, 1997
When I lift up my eyes to behold the skies,
My first thoughts are of Heaven,
I think how it is going to be,
When I see Jesus, my soul is going to be free.
No more sickness, no heartaches, no sorrow to bear-
I would love to say I shall miss all my "dear hearts"
When I get up there,
All of that is up to my savior,
About those prayers I'm not clear
He will make all decisions.

Sometimes I imagine I see Him poring over a huge tome,
It seems He just scratched out a name,
I say, "Oh please, Jesus, not my name, I so do want to come Home!"
I do want to be alert enough to still tell everyone I meet to seek His love.
They need to know if they don't accept Him as Savior,
They will have **NO** eternity with Jesus above.

So I ask, "Do you know Jesus?"
Do you know what a Friend you can have in Him?
No, He does not make everything perfect for you,
But you can rest in His promises in whatever you do.
Then someday, when it's time,
About His heart you will learn.
Because everything will be perfect,
His reasons you will discern.
What a friend you can have in Jesus!
He already loves you,
But you know it takes two!

Fire Up

Precious Jesus, hold my hand while I am praying,
That I may feel Your power while I am saying,
"I love you with all of my heart, you are forever and ever dear,
I want to feel Your Holy Presence always very near.
Here on earth we must keep our fire for You flaming oh so high,
Blazing our love and praise just like lightning in the sky.
Lukewarm love for You will never be sufficient,
You know each and every heart for You are The Omniscient.
Help us Jesus to fire up our hearts anew,
So much heat that you will feel our love rising,
Straight up there to You."
Help us Jesus!
Amen

Count It All Joy

I thank my God every time I remember
That I have chosen Him to be the Lord of my life.
Having Him in charge saves a lot of sorrow
Through many times of strife.
I count it all to joy!

Even in hardships we can feel joy, it comes from inward strength.
If we have Christ within us we can go to most any length.
I have so much love for Him in my heart,
I know that He will never, never from me depart.
I count it all to joy!

I know of late I cry a lot, whenever my Jesus of speak,
His love has so deeply softened my heart, but it has never made me weak.
I delight in telling others how He saved a wretch like me.
Why don't you ask Jesus-right now- to come and save you?
He will do it, just ask Him, His love for you is so true.
I count it all to joy!

He arose!
We are coming into a joyful celebration.
For our sins, God sent His precious Son to die,
The wonder of it all, it was to save us.
Believe it, now we never HAVE to die. It's awesome.
Count it all joy!

Jesus arose from His grave, and He is living.
He will be coming back again,
Don't wait even one moment, call Jesus.
He is longing to hear from you.
Yes, you can go Home on High with Him!

I'm looking forward to going with Jesus.
What a glorious day that will be,
When we all get to Heaven
And live with Him eternally.
No wonder I count it all joy!
I Love You, Jesus.

Which Way Will You Go?

I know there is a Glory road just across the way.
Yes, there are some potholes and tolls we have to pay.
But mostly it's smooth riding and ends up paved in gold,
I know it's true, we can believe the greatest story ever told.
When you come to the crossroads, and the road signs are there,
One is Glory Road, but the other is Satan's Lair.
Dear ones, please stay on Glory Road, the other is a dead end,
On Glory road you will find Jesus, to your path He will attend.
He will guide you safely home to Glory,
He is a wonderful, loving friend.

Me, I want to travel the Glory Road,
It runs straight and true.
I'll find my Jesus at the end of it,
He is there, waiting for me and for you!

Tell Them

Here on Earth morality is disintegrating,
Woe unto us if we just sit around waiting.
For things to get better? Here? No way!
We need to step up and help our brothers and sisters today.
Tell them about Jesus, He is The Way.
Tell them to say "no" to abortion.
Stop taking little babies lives,
They will never forgive themselves,
Even if it is all legalized.
Tell them to guard their children,
To raise them in God's word.
Tell them often that He loves them,
The sweetest message ever heard
Tell them that Jesus died on a Cross,
To pay for all our sin,
Tell them that from a grave He arose,
And He is coming back again.
Tell them to repent, accept, and trust Jesus,
Always walking by His side.
There are trials, we all have them,
But with the help of Jesus, we are able to abide.
So glorify our Lord Jesus! Say "yes" to the Truth!
Perhaps the time of great rebellion
Against God is drawing nigh.
Then the evil one will come,
So wicked and so sly.
As horrible as it is going to be,
Hold on to the Truth and His love,
For Jesus is going to overcome His foe,
And take us to our special Home above.
Tell them! Please!

-3-
The End of Jo's Journey

Jo knew her days on God's earth was nearing an end. She dreamed about what her life would be like after her death. You could even say that Jo fantasized about it. There was no doubt in her mind where she was spending eternity. <u>My First Day in Heaven</u> is the perfect end to a perfect journey for a follower of Christ.

Lately

Lately, sorrowful thoughts come in and crowd my sleep
In the middle of the night
It's a very lonely feeling to lie awake
And wonder why this old heart doesn't feel just right.
Yet, it is late in the night and late in my life,
And I just don't know what is really bothering me.
Oh, but I know someone who is never sleeping,
I can call and talk to Him, you see!

No, I don't hear Him speak,
But His Presence I can always feel.
I am awe-stricken when I think of Him,
As on my knees I kneel.
With much digression I ramble on,
Speaking of everything in my heart,
Our Lord is so magnificent, He listens to even tho'
He knows it all from the start.
Seems it is all about my seventy plus years,
 Now I know when no longer on this earth I trod,
 I will be secure in Heaven with God.
The problem, I have concluded,
After my talk with Him you see
Is whether I can make reservations for everyone
I want to take you up there with me.
Alas, I can take no one
All have to make plans on their own.
So dear loved ones get your plans laid,
You too can make Heaven your eternal home,
Accept Our Father's invitation
Soon and very soon is not to fast.
I pray I will meet you all in Heaven
When our lives down here are past.
Amen

Tomorrow?

Tomorrow, who knows, will there even be a tomorrow?
What is our life?
A mist that appears for a little while
And then vanishes. (James 4:14)
If it's the Lord's will,
We will have a tomorrow.
If it's not,
That "mist" may mean sorrow.
So it's today,
Our plans <u>must</u> be for today!
If you don't know Jesus as your Savior,
Call on Him right away.
He is always near,
He will always hear.
Pray:
> "Jesus, I need you, do you hear my plea?
> I confess I'm a sinner, please forgive me,
> I accept You as my Savior, please accept me!"

Jesus will do it!
He loves you so much,
Just trust in Him
And your soul He will touch.
Then tomorrow will be forevermore,
When at last we all meet on Heaven's golden shore.

So call Him.
Call Him right now.
Don't wait.
Trust in Jesus,
Don't let it be too late.

Please call Him – NOW!

Red Light

Dear Lord, when I walk in my own willful way,
Deep in my heart I hear you say,
"Careful, walk My way!"
Lord, when my wicked tongue gossips today
Again from my heart I hear you say,
"Careful, don't gossip, you better pray!"
Lord, when my anger burns up my good fuel,
Again, there you are,
"Careful, don't be Satan's tool!"
Lord, in my heart I do have "Your Light."
Careful is yellow, I must keep that in sight.
But Lord, how I love you, and Your Words I have read,
When of any sin I am tempted,
      Please, let "Your Light", always flash "RED".

What A Sunset!
March 1993

Not long ago just by chance (or maybe not), I beheld a sunset that was so extraordinarily beautiful I thought it was painted just for me. Sure, I have seen lovely sunsets, but I can't recall one before that overwhelmed me with a feeling of such joy. No "painting" has ever done that until now! How great Thou art God! How much proof do we need to have that You are Supreme and You are the Master of all works? Is it plagiarism then? I know God did it first! If I had not been a believer, that sunset would surely have started a search for truth. The truth is the Bible. We can believe it! I do. Do you?

I'm adding a poem here, it's part of an old hymn, I'm sure. Oh, how I wish I had written this one, but alas it belongs to someone named Haldor Lillenas. Christians can, with confidence, know these words are true.

"The Bible stands like a rock undaunted
'Mid the raging storms of time;
Its pages burn with the truth eternal,
And they glow with a light sublime.

The Bible stands though the hills may tumble,
It will firmly stand when the earth shall crumble;
I will plant my feet on its firm foundation,
For the Bible stands."

Isn't that powerful? More proof of all this is Psalm 119:89, "Forever, O Lord, Thy Word is settled in Heaven."
I'm planting my feet on the firm foundation of my Bible.
Please come stand by me!
Love,
Jo Chamberlain

My Choice Is Made

How I sing of my Redeemer,
For all things He has promised me.
The sting of death cannot destroy me,
My soul in my Savior's care will be!
I'll be living up in Heaven,
In a "place" prepared for me.
You too can have your own "place",
Just accept Jesus as your Savior,
Live with Him eternally.
Imagine! Life in Glory-
Not a worry, not a care!
Safe in the arms of Jesus,
Nevermore to know despair.
Yes, I plan to go up to Glory,
For Jesus I do so want to see.
Please, why don't you make Him your choice?
Come on! Go with me!

"A Merry Heart Doth Good Like A Medicine"
(Proverbs 17:22)

Jesus has put so much love in my life,
He has indeed given me a merry heart.
I believe He wants me to pass on a smile,
And sometimes a little joke to impart.
I love to do this for someone who is "down"
Sometimes humor can chase away a frown.
Humor in some situations can help soften woe,
Also I can smile and tell everyone,
"Jesus loves you so."
To do this always gives me much pleasure,
for my Saviors love is my hearts treasure.
You too can have a merry heart,
Glumness is no virtue, you know,
So let your merry spirit make someone happy
Everywhere you go!
As for me, on an "off" day, I'll use His medicine.
With a merry heart I'll doeth good,
I'll give someone a happy grin.

Still Praising

I could by now have used up the years promised to me,
I'm still praising my Savior, He is so precious to me.
Tho, I'm just a little reluctant to leave this Earth,
Until I can first give Jesus everything He is worth.
That choice I don't have,
In His time He will choose.
One thing I know, in His love I can't lose!
Do you know Jesus?
He is the best "Thing" that could happen to you.
If He taps on your hearts door, please let Him come in
He loves you and He is waiting to forgive all your sin.
Please accept Jesus right now, do not delay.
Give Jesus His glory and in His love – stay!
Jesus is longing to hear from you.
His line is open, you can always get through.
I did! Will you? Please hurry!
"May all who seek You rejoice and be glad in You." Psalm 70:4

Always Praise Him

I feel a great need to praise Our Lord
For all things He has brought me through
Tho' I'm not worthy of His care
For anything I do.
Hallelujah! Praise the Lord!
I would be happy to think I put a smile
Upon His loving face
Everytime I thank Him for His Blessing,
And for His overflowing Grace.
Hallelujah Lord! I love You!
Let us all praise Him for His Presence
In our walk on Earth with Him –
Hallelujah! Lord we praise you!
Hallelujah! Amen.

Help Me Lord

Now and then I fall back to an old sin of worrying after prayer.
Why can't I just remember Our Lord is eternally dependable?
For us He is always there!
He holds us by our right hand,
We need not be afraid,
Mere men cannot hurt us, that is a promise that He made.
Another sin that we should be aware of,
Is being quickly provoked in our spirit.
Anger is a tool that satan uses,
As for me, I really fear it!
Yes, I often do become angry.
I'm the fool whose "lap anger hangs out in".
I pray to the Lord to forgive me, and His pardon I know I will win.
We must trust God completely, put Him first in all we do.
He is the Only One who can stay the slay the devil,
And He is wonderfully able to see us through.
Do you trust Him? Take His hand!
Let Him guide you through this land.
I know when time here on Earth is o'er
He will be watching and waiting for us up on Heaven's shore.

Last Stop

When our loves are seemingly not going so well,
We can count on Satan to pop up with his old "show and tell".
He will promise us anything, his tongue bursting with lies,
Don't believe him, dear friend, he is death in disguise.
Do you know my friend Jesus, our God's only Son?
He paid for all sin!
For us He died on a cross,
So special was Jesus, many people cried, "what a loss!"
Oh, but in just three days, up from a grave He arose,
What a victorious triumph over all of His foes.
He taught love, faith, and trust in Our Father for some thirty years.
Then His departure up to God brought on many tears.
However, He promised to come back one day,
To gather up all who believe He is the way.
Me? I believe! I wonder, what about you?
Pray to Our Father, confess to Him all your sin,
He will forgive you, trust Him.
He is coming back again!
Heaven will be our last stop,
When Jesus comes back again!

Please Lord

Please Lord, lock Your love into my heart.
That I may never from Your side depart.
Please instill in that heart a love like Yours,
That transcends all others,
That I may share everything,
With all my sisters and my brothers.
I was made, not as perfect, but in Your mold,
Let me help You find Your lost lambs,
And bring them humbly into Your fold.
So please Lord, lock Your love into my heart,
And let me make a difference.

"Remember Now Your Creator In The Days Of Your Youth"
(Ecclesiastes 12:1)

God is with us wherever we go.
We are warned to be aware of now and always judgment, you know.
Remember God and do all things, as you know He wants you to,
We never know if our days will be many or few.
Oh, how like a dreadful storm it will be,
If we have lived without hope, faith, and love.
To remember that the day of death will come
With judgment from up above.
In such a storm the sun, moon, and stars go dark,
The clouds come back after the rain.
Everything is so very dreary, our hearts will fill with pain.
The mills stop grinding the flour and the meal.
The silence is frightening, everyone runs for cover.
Everything is so very still.
So remember to accept God as your Savior,
In the days of your youth is best,
Before the silver cord of life has snapped.
And your days have become meaningless.
Please remember your Creator – right now!

Call

It's so wonderful to rise in the morning
At the first light of the day.
To call out to Our Father, and bid Him come my way.
Of course He comes, He is always near,
We must invite Him in.
The serenity of His Presence!
What a way for my day to begin!
I thank Him for His loving kindnesses
And all His blessings sent my way.
I thank Him for the Holy Spirit,
My Helper every day.
I thank Him for my Savior Jesus
For my salvation, He did pay!
What a pleasure to spend this time with God
In the stillness of an early day.
What is your favorite time with Our Father?
A good choice is any hour at all.
He is always waiting and listening –
Just to receive your call.
Please call Him!

Come Now

Come young people, come to Jesus now.
"I'll never forsake you;" He made that vow.
Many of you think, "Then we can't have any fun,"
Now that's an untruth if I ever heard one.
Where is it written that Jesus hates fun?
It's all part of life, tho' not number one!
His eyes will twinkle when you're having fun.
His love will comfort you when tears have begun.
So, come young people and trust Jesus today,
He will give you the best life, with time to "play"!

What A Deal

It's been just a brief moment, dear Jesus, in Your time,
But here on Earth, it's been almost six years in mine.
I still praise you, my Savior, for turning my life around,
My love for You will always abound.
Now, I must tell everyone for my love to be true,
"Please seek Jesus, and He will always find you,
Accept Him as your Savior, and your life will be new,
All trials are not gone, but He will see you through.
Oh, what a bargain, your salvation is free,
Then you live with Jesus throughout eternity."

Only Trust Jesus

Would you agree that we should be spending ever more time in prayer?
The presence of Satan is frightening and it's felt just everywhere.
We can't possibly see him lurking behind every single tree,
He is there tho', you can be sure of it, stalking you and stalking me.
What does Satan really care about us?
He wants only to destroy us in time.
If you do what he wants, he will promise you great things,
Every single time.
Don't you believe him, he is a liar!
Never give up your walk with Jesus,
To end up in a lake of fire.
Do not let yourself be put in that circumstance,
Nothing, absolutely nothing is worth taking that chance.
Keep on loving the Lord, trust only in Him,
He will command His angels to guard you in all your ways,
He knows if you truly love Him, He will protect you all your days!
The most beautiful thing is that at the end of our life on Earth story –
We will be living forever with Jesus,
And our home will be in Glory!

Be Still

All through the Bible we are commanded that our God we must fear.
More than being "afraid," reverent respect for God is alive here!
Overwhelming awe in His presence is needed,
I truly felt, with all my love for Him,
With His command I had succeeded.
Not enough! Sometimes I look away from God and focus on me.
Don't you just know this fills the devil with glee?
I pray that I will always quickly remember,
That my life is in Gods hands.
My priorities must be to love Him
And to obey His commands.
Nothing here belongs to me! Talent? Money? No!
All was afforded by Him to me,
He really does love me so!

No Need For Panic

Now and then I feel I'm slipping,
That on my Rock I've lost my foothold.
I anticipate the worst of things,
Even my heart feels numb and cold.
I'm not perfect like Our Savior,
Sometimes I feel I've lost His favor.
That's enough to cause these problems
For the weak and maybe even the bold.
It's panic!
There is not panic in Heaven,
Because Jesus is in charge up there.
Here, we panic when we read or see the news,
"Please Jesus, don't let that happen here."
We panic in a thunderstorm when lightning comes too near.
Even behind our locked doors we panic,
Where unexpected noises we hear.
Panic! Panic! On Earth there are so many things to fear.
There is no panic in Heaven with Jesus,
So, why don't we let Him be in charge down here?
A crown of thorns He has already worn for us,
As they took Him to the cross
To die that we might live.
He lives again! It's our turn! Let's give Him everything we can give,
There is no need for panic with Jesus in charge!

It's Your Choice

Be still and listen! Jesus could be whispering your name,
If you answer His call with, "I hear you Jesus,"
I tell you, your live just cannot stay the same.
I remember I always heard about Jesus,
Yet, I thought of the Bible as just another book to read.
No sinner wants a book to tell them of a life they need to lead.
This Book is different, down deep in ones' heart one just knows that it is all true.
It was written for everyone on Earth, He knows us all by name.
Many people have excuses for not reading it,
These excuses are so very lame.
Some people say, "How can He be a loving God,
In the world crime and evil always seems to have the upper hand?"
God says, "Punishment for all us coming. Be patient!"
His perfect timing could be near at hand.
Some also say, "Oh, if He is so very loving,
Why would He send anyone to hell?"
He does NOT just Do that!
In His word (if one reads it), we have choices,
I know that very well!
If someone does not choose Heaven,
The only other choice is hell.
So, dear one, read God's Word,
You will learn of His beautiful Rest.
A wonderful choice really can be yours,
God's promises to you are the best.
Today is the right time to find peace with Him,
Tomorrow may be too late.

Happy Anniversary With Love

(This poem was written for Pastor Dave and Jan Bohyer in celebration of their twenty-five years of marriage. It was read at our church (Grace Evangelical) picnic at Wing Park in Elgin. In August 1995. It would be such a blessing if they could always be with us at Grace. I tell you everybody loves Pastor Dave and Jan.)

We are all so delighted to celebrate with our Pastor Dave and our First Lady Jan,
Their twenty five years of being together,
Living out Our Gods marriage plan.
We know everything many not have been perfect,
But by loving each other and following God's command –
We are able to know they were truly led by Our Masters Hand.

Pastor Dave and Jan have been at Grace, I believe it has been about five years or so.
It was great fun to watch their wonderful sons, Mark, Micah, and Daniel grow.
Those young men have done many special things,
And oh, they are so very good.
It proves that having such a caring Mom and Dad,
Leads young people to do as they should.

Did you know Pastor is an early riser?
Do you think he takes early walks?
Do you think he puts his serpents on a leash?
And as they walk along, do they listen as he talks?
I think maybe they give him clues on how to handle their "kind-"
Say, maybe that's why he is so terrific at kicking Satan's behind?!

Now – do you know about Jan, she likes to sleep late?
I think her loveliness is due to all that!
But here's what I say, and maybe you think like me,
If I could be as lovely as Jan, I would sleep until three (p.m.).
I don't want all this to get out of hand –
So lets just wish our Pastor Dave and our Jan –
A Happy, Happy Anniversary!
"Please Father in Heaven, guard them on Earth
All of their remaining days –
As they are busy turning hearts and souls to You
In very special ways.
We here at Grace treasure them so much
And while they are in this land –
Please Father, we pray they will always
Feel the Touch of Our Masters Hand."

Amen

This poem was written for Jo's music pastor's son on his 1st birthday.

For A Little Denton: Jefferson

To Our most Precious Father, I pray-
That You will grant me a very special prayer today.
I have a sweet little friend, yes-
And I neglected to ask Your blessings for him.
I'm so sorry and it was on his very first birthday-
So Lord, please shower him with Your perfect love in every way.
You will do it now I pray. We call him our little J.J.
In his life, please allow him all the things he will need-
And guard him all his days. In Jesus sweet name these things I plead.
I love you.
Your servant,
Jo chamberlain

Remember God Hates Sin, He Loves You

Sin is the beginning of a pernicious spreading evil.
Sin can lead you down a road that leads only to despair.
Or you can call on Jesus to come save you,,
Call Him, Jesus will always be there!
He is listening now as I ask for His help.
"Oh Lord, as we live through another year,
We must not leave too many things undone.
Bringing new souls to You Lord,
Should be our priority number one.
Please lead us to hearts that are breaking,
We can tell them You can lift their load.
Lead us with compassion to hearts that feel,
That for them, there is no other road.
Help us Lord, we must not discriminate,
As we reach out to sisters and brothers.
The color of a face makes no difference,
The love in that heart is the same as all others.
Lord, please help us, if we just pass on by,
Some seemingly very needful stranger,
And after we have passed – without stopping,
We find out it was an angel in danger.
Lord, help us to find souls that have gone back to sin,
We must get their hearts throbbing for You again.
It's urgent we make haste with these hearts today,
Satan already has them heading swiftly down another way.
Please Lord, help us to save little babies,
Some have no choice whether to live or to die.
Help us to make a difference in that, Lord.
It only can happen if we zealously try.
Lord, help us here in America.
Just as in Isaiah's time, righteousness seems to stand afar.
Therefore, justice is driven back.
Honesty has stumbled in our country,
Truth cannot get on the right track.
Oh, Dear Lord, You are the real truth, and You are the real way.
Come help us Lord, help us!
We want to save souls for You, every day.

Averse In A Fish

God told Jonah, a prophet, to find a boat and hop it,
To get on down to Nineveh and tell the people,
"Repent of your evil or you will die in our sin!"
Irascible Jonah thought, "No, I don't wanna do that,
I'll just hop a boat to Joppa.
Let someone else tell these jokers how to save their skin!"

So Jonah left Joppa, he was soon on a trading vessel Tarshish bound.
The Lord knew what Jonah was up to, so He sent a violent storm upon the sea.
Every single sailor on board that vessel said,
"We're going to drown, can it really be?"
So, quickly they went below deck and found prophet Jonah snoring,
They sensed the end was near because the rain was greatly pouring.
So, they awakened Jonah and told him to ask his God to save them.
No! Jonah wouldn't do it, he was still trying to run from Him.

When the wind roared louder and the waves got even higher,
The sailors asked, "What should we do to you to calm the sea down?"
Jonah finally answered, "Pick me up and throw me in it, I know I'm to blame the most.
The pagan sailors were kinder than Jonah,
They would not do that.
They tried their best to row him back to the coast.
Guess what?
It was like a miracle the pagan sailors called out to our Lord to help "them".
As they made vows to our Lord,
They threw Jonah over the rail and out to sea, and the sea grew still.
In the stillness a big, big fish came sailing by,
And sucked up Jonah with a sigh.
It was not accidental – it was Gods will.

(Inside the fish) It's Jonah:
"Why didn't I do what the Lord told me to do?!

See, now I'm going to end up in a pot of fish stew!
Why couldn't I just have cruised on over there and preached to those losers?
It wasn't all that much He asked me to do!
God does all the saving with His mercy and grace
All He told me to do was go and preach in that place.
There are ugly googley eyes flashing all around in here,
What can I do? Look at me now!
I feel like I'm sittin' in a bowl full of jelly –
And even worse than that, there are creepy crawly things all over my belly."
Right then and there Jonah called out to the Lord to come and save him.
Our Lord is so constant and loving, as He lifted up His hand,
   He told the fish, "Kindly just spit Jonah up on the sand."

God spoke to Jonah about Nineveh again,
"Go there and warn them of impending doom because of their sin."
This time Jonah hustled off and gave them the Word,
The Ninevites repented just as soon as they heard.
We too can simply proclaim to others, about God, what we know-
We may be surprised to find out how much interest they show.

God showed His compassion for the sinners and forgave them.
His purpose is correction not revenge.
Jonah wanted to die because the Ninevites accepted Gods call,
The Lord asked him if he had any right to be upset about it at all!

Jonah had made himself a shelter as he awaited the outcome of the city.
The most happening in that shelter was a lot of self-pity.
The Lord provided a vine overhead to cool him fine,
Next day He also provided a worm to kill the vine.
At the loss of his vine Jonah was angry again,
But not at what would have happened if Nineveh was still into sin.
But was concerned about so many people and such a great city,

We cry when we lose a loved one,
And show lots of friends our pity.
Shouldn't we also cry when sinners die?
And their souls don't belong to Our Lord?
God saved many people in the Book of Jonah
Whey they asked for His mercy and aid –
There was Jonah, the sailors, and all of Nineveh
God was there, right there, as soon as they prayed.

God is here too:
When we hear, see, and read about our own America today,
In B.C. Assyria things could have been just the same way.
It's probably not any better here in nineteen ninety five,
Then it was in those days when Jonah was alive.
We need God's mercy and judgement because of our population,
As much now, if not more than we did then
No matter how we rate some little things,
God calls a SIN-A SIN!

It took a miracle of deliverance to get Jonah to do what God told him to do –
Let that be a lesson for me, and yes for you.
So when God tells us, "Do it," let's just hop right up to it.
We can follow in His footsteps all the way!

Oh Lord, You Seasoned The Earth

Oh Lord, after the winter, then comes the springtime,
Another season that just bursts in delight.
The good Earth You made brings forth Your glory,
The sun says, "Good Morning," it's so golden and bright.
Yes, also comes the rain drops to sparkle after the rain.
To cleanse the winters tear drops and wash away pain.
Oh Father, Thank You for Your Love, it shows in the beauty –
There is the delicate rose, with its scent oh so sweet,
All the green things You designed makes a background that is heart halting and so complete,
Oh God, how did You make those little brooks ripple and sing,
And how did you teach all the little birds to grow and take wing?
Lord, even Your streaking lighting and Your echoing thunder,
Seem just a little threatening but they are so breath catching and so thrilling.
Oh yes, when truth is told, the excitement is a little bit chilling.
Oh God, we love You so much,
And You do make exciting masterpieces for all seasons
In our hearts we adore all of them.
For possibly, different reasons.
With all of our artists and all of their "arts,"
Your "works" are the ones that really "fire" up our hearts,
For all of us know that most masterpieces on Earth have to be copies,
Most of us must know that not much could be as lovely as a field of Your red poppies.

For all of us now, I pray that our hearts will beat faster –
When we stand in awe of the "works" of Our Master.
When paintings are signed on this Earth that we trod –
May our hearts take wing at the ones signed – God.
Lord, put your brush marks on our hearts!

Have You Talked to My Friend?

Over all my way Jesus leads me,
He knows exactly where I am.
Now I'm not always as grateful as I should be
Doesn't that just prove what a sinner I still am?
Yes, I know He can handle all things,
And He will handle my needs in His time.
When I think of how many souls that must need Him, at this very moment,
Then I'm content to wait upon mine.

He gives us power to grow through our trials and woe,
Experiencing problems can build character, perseverance, and sensitivity toward others, we know.
Our troubles could be a sign of effective Christian living, I pray.
That thought makes it all a joy, living for Jesus each day.

The "Tempter" is always trying to get inside my head,
But I keep Jesus inside my heart,
And He will help me with a "be gone!"
And Satan will quickly depart.
It's not easy without Jesus, we can't make it on our own,
Please ask Jesus to be your Savior,
Then you will never, ever, be alone.
Go ahead say, "Jesus please come by me,
I want you for my Own."
Ask His forgiveness for your sins
He has already paid for.
Yes, for all our sins He died to atone.
So please call on Him, He is so alive today,
I tell you He will help you. He is the Way.

As for me, writing this has helped me too,
I'll remember to be more grateful for everything He brings me through.
I love you Jesus!

America Is Still Free

We thank you Father for all the brave men and women that have given their lives on the battlefields, so America could still be free.
We pray that all our gallant heroes are living up there with Thee.
So many wars have already been, we plead there will be no more.
We really love our America and we want no more wars on any shore.
Lord, there are so many sad memories of lives lost in wars that have gone by.
We surely must have learned some kind of lesson, the cost of World War II was dearly high.
Fighting against our own sisters and brothers was wrong; we should have made them free.
What happened at Pearl Harbor and Hiroshima was a horror; why can't we learn that war is bad?
Will we ever learn from fighting that peace on Earth could be had?
The Holocaust was such a devastation, it was designed by an evil man.
Our dearest Father in Heaven, help us to never let that happen again!
Our Father has written a Book for us on how we should live in this land.
When our life here is over, His Book tells us His final plan.

We thank you Father for this Memorial Day and this chance to remember and thank our fallen heroes.
Speaking of heroes we have Viet Nam veterans who deserve our thanks and our love too.
Oh, dear God, please help them heal their scars, yes, and their wounded hearts too.

Because of our Father, America is still free!

Do We Need A New Wardrobe?

When you dress in the morning, do you pray to be strong for the day?
Do you give your wardrobe a lot of thought; do you dress any certain way?
Everyday we must put on the full armor of God!
The Devil is everywhere with so many plots,
We need to protect our families, and our church,
And keep all saints in our prayers and thoughts.
We need to fight against spiritual forces of evil in heavenly realms
And the powers of this dark world that really got out of bounds.
So in the mornings put on Gods full armor and stand your ground.
Stand! Stand firm! Is the belt of truth buckled around your waist?
Is your breastplate of righteousness firmly in place?
Are your feet fitted with the readiness that comes with the gospel of peace?
Now! Take up your shield of faith to protect you from the arrows that come from the beast.
You are ready!
Take the Word of God, which is the sword of the Spirit and the helmet of salvation.
Be alert! You are ready for battle in any situation,
Pray in the Spirit, always pray for all believers,
You will be prepared for any and all deceivers.
You will all be beautiful in your new attire,
So put on those garments and put out Satan's fire!

The Apostle Paul and Jo Chamberlain,
Servants of Christ Jesus

A Real Gift Of Love

It was a night before Christmas,
On my couch I fell asleep,
Not far from where I slept was a big footrest
And a big old leather chair,
Behind the chair a street light was a backdrop
Like a star shining in over there.
I was awakened, I thought, by a sound
Like someone whispering, "I am here."
Quickly I sat up and toward the chair did peer.
I knew in an instant someone was near
So I said, "Is that you Santa, are you taking a break?"
A soft voice answered,
"Come listen to me if you are truly awake,"
I moved close enough to see His eyes,
And tears there I saw glistening,
"I'm a little like Santa, but I'll tell you who I am,
If you are really listening."
He said, "I am Jesus, I've come to ask you a favor,
Please tell everyone you meet about Me
And how their love I would savor."
Tell them their greatest Christmas gift could be life everlasting.
"But yes, there is something from them I am asking.
They must call upon Me and confess all their sin,
I have a gift of forgiveness that is promised to them.
Tell them to ask and they will receive.
I, unlike Satan, can never deceive."
As I listened my heart was filled with so much love,
On my cheek I felt a soft touch,
Like a big furry glove.
I was struggling to see Him,
Tho' in my heart I knew He was gone.
I opened my eyes, and oh, the love lingered on.
Yes, He has left, but He has not gone very far.
Just call upon Him and He will meet you where you are.

Birth Of Our Messiah

"In 1990 I made a special Christmas card and sent it to Grace Church – in care of Jesus. This is the poem I wrote for that card."
Jo

One starry night for a shining hour,
Heaven touched Earth,
And angels proclaimed a special birth –
"It's a Baby Boy, called Jesus!"
He came down here bearing a gift for us.
Some people didn't know and some didn't care.
All these years later, we here at Grace,
Know what He had to share.
It's Christmas!
Let us all pass His Gift along to everyone with joy.
And celebrate the birth of that Holy Baby Boy, Jesus!

He Is Love

I was so aware of the Presence of the Greatest Love of my heart.
'Twas not the first time I've felt it,
Tho' it always gives me a "jump start".
It stemmed from being reminded of what Christmas is really all about.
Not parties, nor presents –
It's Jesus only Jesus!
In my heart and mind, there is not any doubt.
I pray for people who don't believe or care about our King.
Never will they know that He is the Joy that makes your soul sing.
Tho' we may have hardships, pain and sorrow,
Always lean on Jesus for a better tomorrow!
One day <u>no</u> tomorrow is going to rise,
But we have the promise of a new Home up there in His lovely blue skies.
His Promise!
Dear Hearts, This Great Presence was felt on "Bah, Humbug" Sunday.
I tell you Jesus is the Truth and the Real Love.
Give Him a chance; you'll see!

The Manger And The Cross

Was there a shadow from the Cross protecting the Baby in that manger?
Did it at that time secure Jesus from being found, and in great danger?
All Glory to God for His sacrifice so dear,
The Messiah had arrived, Our Savior was here.
A tiny precious Baby had come to save a world full of sinners.
And when Satan challenged Jesus, he found out Jesus was the winner.
Jesus was so faithful, so loving, and true,
He gathered up His disciples, maybe me, maybe you!?
Oh the joy of knowing you are working for Our King.
Doesn't that beautiful thought just make your heart sing?
At this Christmas season, remember the birth of Jesus is what Christmas is all about!
Think about it, think long about it,
Really, you can just hear your heart shout!
If you did not have that joy, Jesus wants to give you that gift.
Seek Him, call Him, open your door.
He will come in if you invite Him,
And your heart will sing forever more.

We love you Jesus, Happy Birthday!

Oh, Happy Day

The morning of my birthday came up with a beautiful sun,
I knew then, that the joy had already begun.
Soon we were off to "Grace" looking forward
To a special message by Todd.
It was so good, he reminded us how we are
Wanted and longed for by Our Father above.
My first delight came as I looked around and I felt my heart lurch.
As my eyes beheld all the people sitting there filling up our church. Amen!

After all the fun of greeting and hugging was o'er,
We were back home again and as I walked in my door,
I said, "That was great God, can I really expect more?"
"Will any 'one' of those wonderful people come knock on my door?"
forgive me, Dear Lord, me of so little trust,
I should have known –
You sent those beloved guests, for a special birthday they are a "must"!
It was so exciting, my home was just full.
They showed so much, I felt like a genuine "JEWEL".
And then Lord, I heard a celestial choir.
They were singing "Happy Birthday."
I felt lifted so high, and my heart burned like a candle.
The "little dance" was for You, I guess my years fell away.
And myself I just couldn't handle,
Where I came back down from Heaven,
I just knew You had been here.
I'll remember this birthday and all of the cheer,
You have fulfilled Your promise even if this is my last year.
However, most Precious Father, what I want most of all –
Is to be a good, faithful servant, until You <u>do call</u>!
Thank You again for my party, my good friends, my family and Your love,
I'm telling everybody, "All good things truly come from above."
I love You Lord.

What Do You Say?

The holidays have really been sort of heart stopping,
Too many parties, too much food,
And most of all, the "killer shopping"!
Now that we are into nineteen ninety eight –
Now that we have too little time and too much strife,
Why don't we dare to be different in our life?
Let's just – "Let Go and Let God!"

Celebrating the birth of Our Savior, is a very special time –
We start out with a great desire to praise Him,
But do we get so busy that we leave Him behind?
We need to remember that long, long ago,
Our Father asked Jesus if He would go and die,
To pay for our sin.
With very little hesitation, Jesus did say "yes" –
There and then

Now we must open our heart's door
And bring Him back in.
I know not everyone was guilty of this,
But I, for one, feel much remorse.
Now I want to let go and let God choose my course.
What do you say?

The Walk
(Psalm 91)

I dreamed I took a walk with Jesus,
It was on a quiet road, I know not where.
I could not imagine why this happened,
Where were we going, why was I even here?
Then I heard His voice, ever so softly, tenderly say –
"Jo, do you remember how I told you,
If you make the Most High your dwelling,
You will never come to harm?
Do you remember I said I would command my angels
To guard you in all your ways?
They will lift you up and protect you from evil
Through all your days.
Do you remember, I said, because you love Me
I will rescue you, when you call Me I will answer?
Something, even more, will be your jubilation,
When I show you My Salvation!"

Slowly I awakened and peeked, I thought I might
Find myself in another Place.
But no – so, I still have another pleasure.
I'll just keep on serving here at Grace.
It was a glorious dream!
To everyone who reads this:
You too can walk with Jesus, perhaps He will call you today,
Don't let His call go unanswered –
He is the only Way!
Please! Take the Walk.

The Rain Will Dry Up-So Should We!

Oh Lord, we are complainers, please forgive us when we just sit around and carp-
We could, instead, spend our time as Your Angels did, learning to play a harp.
But no, we lounge around saying, "Oh boy, it's just too hot."
Or it's "Gee, is Noah on the way, it's raining an awful lot?"
But, then too, we say, "Last winter was just too cold, it brought on all these aches and pains, makes me feel I'm getting old!"

My First Day In Heaven

I found myself walking on cool white sand,
I just kept moving along viewing the land.
Very soon I saw a gorgeous blue sea,
Somehow I just knew it was the Sea of Tranquility.
Then turning around I saw a huge Golden Gate,
I rang a little tinkling bell and stood there to wait.
Soon the gate swung open and I saw a big smiling man,
You guessed it, it was Peter and he took my hand.
But another man said, "Wait, she's probably in the wrong place."
Peter said, "Oh Thomas, must you always doubt?
She was invited here by Jesus,
That's what this is all about."

As I walked in the gate my heart began to sing,
Soon, I knew I was going to see My King.
Dr. Luke came over to check up on me,
He said, "Now your heart is healed, you are really Home free."
Someone said, "I thank my God every time I remember you,"
I turned around, I just knew it was Paul,
His "thorn" was gone, God had made him brand new.
I said, "Later," to the apostles, "I'll see you around."
Paul was my escort,
We were off to see the sights in this Glorious Town.

Imagine we walked on streets paved with gold!
Suddenly it seemed normal to just do this, I remember being told.
We would be living in splendor among things
Made of diamonds, jasper, and gold.
It was so serene as we strolled,
I met Joshua, Samuel, Daniel, and Ruth.
Believe it, everything as is written
In our Bible is truth.

Just a little farther on I saw a lush green space,
I sauntered right on down to look at the place.
Guess what?!
There was a ballgame going on.
I saw Moses hit the ball with a real "hard whack."
Moses made the base, but he broke the bat.
I'm sure the Lord must have smiled when He saw the bat swing,
He remembered Moses in a former "thing."
Then along came Job.
I asked him if he had a message for people down on Earth,
What words would he choose?
He said, "Tell them:
Patience! Trust Jesus! Satan will lose!"
It was time! Paul said, "Jo, we really must go,
Someone Else is waiting to see you, don't you know?"
Oh, I felt my heart and soul
Thundering in delight.
And then I saw "it"!
A mansion in gold and diamonds, glistening ever so bright.

There was a hush, everything seemed so Holy,
At the same time I saw a door opening ever so slowly.
My joy was complete when I saw His nail scarred hand,
And I heard a beautiful voice say,
"Welcome Home, Jo, you are in Beulah Land!"

I'm Home at last! Jesus is waiting for all of you too.
He's eagerly watching and longing for you.
The door in <u>your</u> mansion is standing ajar,
Please come give your heart to Jesus, He's not very far!

"I would like to thank Jeff for giving me this challenge. I loved doing it, and I pray everyone will enjoy it. Thanks Jeff!!"

Jo Chamberlain

Written December 1994

I've decided to tell all of you how much I've been blessed by belonging to Jesus, and to Grace Church. Jesus has given me more friends now than I've possibly ever had before. All of you, here! A year ago at this time I had the pleasure of writing an adaptation of Psalm136 for our Thanksgiving service at Elgin Bible Church. A blessing! Just a little later, I was so privileged by being included in the Christmas program, and a special treat of being caroled later. More blessings! Then the Easter program that I shared was another beautiful blessing! Jesus does live!

Now I've found that being here every Tuesday to take care of the pews, is another blessing. I just love doing it. Usually on Tuesday I'm greeted by Todd, or our first lady Jan, or Terri, or Dawn. That's four blessings. Also perhaps our Pastor Dave is going to and fro. He's a blessing!

And let me just tell you that when our own Jeff is playing piano along with Norm Jonsson on the Guitar the place is alive with wonderful music – the blessings are almost more than my heart can take. Thank you, Jesus!

I tell you, get involved with Jesus and the blessings will flow. Try it, you will love it too.

I wish you all peace and Christmas love in Jesus name.

Jo Chamberlain was born in Jefferson County, Illinois on February 15, 1923 to Gertie Lee (Gregory) Garrison and William Alfred Monroe Garrison. She grew up at 522 N. 6th St., Mount Vernon with her siblings Merle, Bob, and Pauline. Jo was raised in a Christian home and she often attended a Baptist church nearby. As a child Jo looked up to and adored her Aunt Dorothy who lived in Ashley. As an adult she looked up to and believed in Jesus and what He stood for. Later in life she moved to Elgin and married Donald Ray Chamberlain. She had three beautiful children: Candy, Craig, and Shelley. Jo's husband was taken from her at a young age leaving Jo to raise their children the best way she could. Jo may not have lived a Christian life but she knew what it meant to be a Christian and raise her children to know Christ. It wasn't until later in her life that Jo became a full believer in Christ. She was baptized in October of 1987.

www.ingramcontent.com/pod-product-compliance
Lightning Source LLC
Chambersburg PA
CBHW051711040426
42446CB00008B/827